Y0-ELT-150

My First 90 Years

DREAMS OF A MILLENNIUM PHILOSOPHER

Sol Goldberg, M.D.

To Rose & Ben Norton,

Two Long Time

" Very Dear Friends".

Best wishes from your

Golfing Buddy,

Sol.

VANTAGE PRESS
New York

The art on the jacket ...
are reproductions of paintings done by the artist Ruth Goldberg, the author's deceased wife. Both have won first place prizes in the Beverly Hills Art League "Affair in the Gardens." The watercolor on the front is untitled; I refer to it as "Baby Wearing a Black Hat." The oil painting on the jacket back is called "Our Three Sons," and represents Sanford, Dennis, and Terry.

FIRST EDITION

Copyright © 2002 by Sol Goldberg, M.D.

Manufactured by Vantage Press, Inc.
516 West 34th Street, New York, New York 10001

Printed in the United States of America

Library of Congress Catalog Card No.: 01-126495

0 9 8 7 6 5 4 3 2 1

This book is dedicated to my beloved deceased wife, Ruth, who was my pal-buddy and life-long companion for sixty-one years until God took her into his domain.

As a youngster, Ruth and her two pals, the La Rue sisters, all beautiful and talented, danced in the operas *Carmen* and *Aida* with Ernest Belcher's Ballet in San Francisco and Los Angeles, California. Ruth excelled in many forms of dancing including toe-tap. She was a true ballerina at an early age.

We married in 1932 during the Great Depression, and we organized a Big Doers club, a frolicking small group. All parties were held in our very tiny one-bedroom apartment with minimum furniture. The members and friends brought their own folding chairs or sat on the floor.

We often danced to the melodies of the old phonograph that still ring in my ears with pleasant memories. We brought happiness to our many friends in those days of uncertainty and shortages, and beyond that time as well.

As a wife and mother, Ruth helped me and our three sons with our professional studies. She was very devoted and bright. Graduation seemed so far off that we thought it would never come.

In my early medical career, Ruth acted as my nurse, and as my practice advanced, she assisted me with my first rhytidectomy [face-lift] procedure. An excellent result was attained.

Ruth started a new career in art and won many prizes. Her paintings are donated and on display in the Dean's Office at the College of Medicine at U.C. Irvine at Cedars-Sinai Hospital, Los Angeles, at U.C.L.A. and U.S.C. I have made greeting cards featuring her prizewinning art, available at this time on the Internet from Amazon.com.

Dedication to the younger generation includes three wonderful sons: Sanford M. [Son Number One] is a noted attorney in Beverly Hills; Dennis I. [Son Number Two] is a prominent physician living in Wyoming; and Terry M. [Son Number Three] is an outstanding attorney in Encino, California.

Their offspring: Bradley, Brian, twins Linda and Lauren, all college graduates, include one physician, two attorneys, and one schoolteacher—author of several outstanding children's books.

Alison, Todd, and Jessica, who are in college and making excellent progress.

Last but not least, our great-grandchildren:

Sarah, Benjamin, and Ethan
Joshua, and Danielle
Lilly and Joy-Rachel
Zach and Lindsay

All are the most brilliant, sweetest, prettiest kids in the world. Wouldn't you expect a great-grandfather to say this?

To Nan Potkin, R.N., Apprentice Pharmacist, my dear friend, whose support and critique in the presentation of this book I hold in highest regard.

A special thanks goes to Alan Simon for the digital rendering of this book for your entertainment.

To Lily Reese: thanks for her able assistance, publicity, and book review.

To my son Dennis: special thanks for his review of this book. He is the author of many books and articles. His latest, called "The Ring," won first prize in the Writers' West quarterly contest.

There are planets within our galaxy that can sustain life. Undoubtedly, they are far different from what we earthly beings know. Perhaps there are many solar systems in which one or more planets exist that resemble our own and have similar characteristics to Earth.

If my belief is correct, we may have distant relatives there to be seen at some future time in space.

—The Millennium Philosopher

Contents

My Poetic Writings

Foreword

There be but one way to describe Sol Goldberg, M.D.—easygoing. As his son, I have never seen him angry, upset, or stressed out except on two occasions. The first was a patient who disturbed the bandages of a keloid scar excision to see my father's fine workmanship of that morning. Unfortunately, this caused trauma to the suture line, which then bled and necessitated Sol spending a portion of his off time repairing the patient's interference.

The other time in which I have seen my dear father distressed was when his beloved, Ruth, passed on. This grief remains to this day substantially diminished with "Tincture of Time." It has also lessened with his penned pages of reader friendly, emotional catharsis in his first book, *a-Word*.

Sol's short dissertations within this second collection also evoke emotions for us all, each in our own way, and with personal interpretation of feelings.

—Dennis I. Goldberg, M.D.

Author's Note

The marvelous experiences I had with my first book, *a-"Word"* in 1997 encouraged me to write this second book, titled *My First 90 Years,* which is a collection of essays, poems, and creative writings about subjects such as *the Soul, Alone,* and *GOD.*

I was invited to present my book to the Book Publicists of Southern California. It was voted the best of the evening and given as a first door prize.

I was invited to meet Mr. Al Gore at the University of California, Los Angeles. He received my book with excellent written comments that I treasure.

I was introduced to Mr. Brad Sherman, Congressman from the San Fernando Valley. He encouraged me to do book signings and interviews in newspapers and radio, which increased my ego.

I did a survey on the word *"Hug,"* and I noted the responses and feelings of people engaged in the act of hugging, including the clergy.

One of the most touching and powerful stories titled *"My Thoughts Now That I Am Alone,"* came to me in the middle of the night. A few days later, I thought what I'd written was so powerful I wanted to burn it.

Author Stanley Bachrack, after reviewing it,

suggested I place it in the first part of this book, as it was excellent. You, the reader, can decide.

"Your Report Card Before GOD" you will find interesting and provocative.

"Wonder" asks the question, "Where were you before you were born?

"Things I Remember At Age Nine Months" demonstrates how important it is for adults to be careful of their conversations and actions in the presence of infants, as they might remember and be affected by negative comments or behavior. Pleasantries are always preferable.

Take life as a game. Produce where you can, be tolerant of others, and you can have a happy life.

Prologue

Words will follow,
with my interpretation and suggestions
for a better life.
It will be humanizing, humorous and
—Educational—
— and even include predictions—
with tongue in cheek.

My First 90 Years

Background

I was born in Brooklyn, New York, 1911. We were a family of two brothers and five sisters. My father, Sam, was rarely home and often absent for months at a time trying to make a living for us. As the eldest son, it behooved me to be in charge of the family at a very early age. Life was not easy.

I had to walk a long distance to school. I remember one winter the only sweater I had was a hand-me-down so large it extended to my ankles. I often went without it even when there was snow on the ground. We moved so frequently that I never had any friends. I really had a difficult childhood. We were so poor.

While I was growing up, I often assisted my father with his business of making prize packages, which were boxes of chewy taffy candies with "a prize in every package." He sold them during intermission in the theaters. Business was improving and I helped him whenever I could.

When I was a senior in high school, my father told me that he had always wanted to be a doctor. Because he was unable to, he wanted me to be one. I said, "Dad, if you want me to be a doctor, I will." With zeal and countless hours of work in numerous jobs

1

and little sleep, I studied and worked my way through school.

My brother-in-law, Max, helped me financially, and so I was able to fulfill our dream.

After graduation I opened a one-dollar clinic in Los Angeles, California, in the depression era. My wife Ruth acted as my nurse. My career changed with years of training in the field of plastic surgery, and I contributed sixteen articles to that field. As my medical practice grew, we were able to take a number of cruises.

I became a Mason and a Shriner and was involved with their wonderful, charitable work. Their burn center is still free to the public.

One night, after a wonderful evening of entertainment, on our entering our home, a gun was thrust at my temple and an arm wrapped around my wife's throat. The robber's demands were met and loot taken.

Two weeks later, on a bright Sunday afternoon, a brazen, young, gun-toting male held us up again. My wife succumbed shortly thereafter from the emotional strain.

Losing my wife to a "gunman" was so traumatic that I was stressed to the point of requiring bypass heart surgery.

We were no longer a couple who worked and played together.

A Brief Note about My Kin

Sam (Samuel), My Father

His father taught him that a man works all his life and must never play. As a young boy, he once played baseball and his father beat him up so badly that he almost killed him, as it was "wrong to play—in life, you work."

As I was a fine golfer and enjoyed it and loved my father, I stopped by Inglewood Country Club at the putting green to putt and insisted that my father try it. He refused at first, but I persuaded him to try. I placed the ball six feet from the cup and gave my dad a putter. To my utter amazement, he sank six putts in a row, much better than I with experience. He threw the club down and said, "No more," recalling his father's comments.

Mom (Sadie), My Mother

Had a beautiful singing voice, was very attentive and devoted her life to her eight children. Her first born, a male, died just after birth in the hospital from an infection caused by a nurse who accidentally pricked his tender skin with a non-sterile safety pin.

Mom cooked for our large family. When Joe, the market man, brought our food to our house each Monday morning, the weeks' supply cost ten dollars.

Mom checked every item to make sure that he did not under-provide. I asked her why she didn't trust him. She said, "It's all the money I have for our family for the week." She was a businesswoman.

My Siblings (*in order of appearance*)

Anne

Anne is my oldest sister and the sweetest person whom I ever knew. She was an all "A" student. Never spoke an evil word about anyone. She was the editor of the U.C.L.A. newspaper. She wrote this story about our uncle Sammy.

"Smile Sammy Smile"

They say that when Sammy was born an angel tapped him on the shoulder and said "Smile Sammy Smile." So Sammy smiled and everyone that looked at him smiled too. But life was not easy for Sammy because often a black cloud came over his face, while his body stiffened and he could not move nor make a sound. His mother twisted her hands in fear. "What's wrong" she cried and screamed, "What's wrong?" "Nothing I'm sure It must have been a cramp" comforted the puzzled nurse as she shook the stiffened child, who finally straightened out. He gave a big grin once more.

(That is how Sammy entered this world.)

A child burdened with Epilepsy-our uncle-cousin.

Dot (Dorothy)

Dot was also an "A" student and was sweet and a very pretty lady. Everything to her was just fine.

Me

This is my place in the family order.

Morton

Skipped several times in school and when Uncle Sam asked for recruits, he was there. Unfortunately, his skull was injured and he has been handicapped since, but he has no regrets.

Mollie

Also an "A" student. Became a teacher and taught privately to the impaired.

Bea (Beatrice)

Very bright. Became a WAVE and an officer in the service.

Pam (Pamela)

She was a beauty. Had a gorgeous voice and sang for the servicemen.

I Remember

My Early Days

You could open a bank account with one dollar. If you had money in the bank, it drew four percent interest.

The newspaper boy on the corner would yell out the current news. He would bring the newspaper to you even from across the street for one cent. A second edition would come out at about 4:00 P.M. and some people would even buy it. An occasional extra with important news was brought out at night. One, I remember, had the heading "World War One." Car horns tooted and people screamed and trembled with fear.

Smog was never present or thought of. The skies were clear with multitudes of stars at night and clouds were blue and white and silvery.

A new Ford or Chevy really cost less than six hundred dollars, and there was no tax. A flat tire was repaired with a cold patch, which everyone knew how to do. Gasoline prices were eight gallons for one dollar, and oil was fifteen cents a quart.

The yellow streetcar allowed three transfers at a cost of five cents. Some passengers had to transfer several times because the tracks did not accommodate each and everyone's direction.

The Red Car would take you from Los Angeles to San Pedro on tracks at high speed.

The movie house cost ten cents. A Harold Lloyd or Charlie Chaplin movie was fifteen cents.

A stick of Wrigley's gum cost one cent or three packages of five sticks for ten cents at the Thifty Drug store. Dinner at their counter cost nineteen cents and included a dessert. An ice cream cone cost five cents—a banana split cost a dime if you had the money.

There was a local price war and milk was two cents a quart, coffee was fifteen cents a pound and a loaf of bread cost two cents.

A new small home and lot in Los Angeles was nineteen hundred and ninety-five dollars with one hundred ninety-five dollars as a down payment. A one thousand dollar life insurance program cost twenty-five cents per week. The agent came around each month to collect one dollar.

The doors to one's house were never locked and a friend might drop in and have a cup of coffee and a doughnut and even leave a thank you note.

It was safe to walk to school unless you ran into the neighborhood bully. You were either his friend or you walked on the other side of the street as you might get punched in the nose, which was his specialty.

The policeman on the corner knew each person

in the neighborhood and would ask about Mom and Dad. He was everyone's friend.

A neighborhood occasionally had two cars racing at twenty-three miles per hour for about one block. Kids played baseball in the streets and had to wait for the occasional auto that went by and would yell to the driver to hurry and get out of the way.

A telephone call was only five cents if Central was awake at the switchboard and the other person on your party line was not using the phone at the same time.

I alternately sold hot dogs or Eskimo pies at the Coliseum for ten cents apiece and walked up and down the bleachers at least one thousand times at each event.

A wristwatch that you wound each night sold for ninety-nine cents. An art gum eraser was used to correct mistakes in spelling. A crystal radio set with cats' whiskers and earphones would get two or three radio stations at the same time.

The Bon Ton Dance Hall on the Santa Monica Pier cost five cents per dance if the girl accepted you.

The Infant with Recall

I remember being in Seattle, Washington, at the age of nine months. My Aunt Sheila wheeled me across the street in a buggy, and we went downhill where there was a theater. She apparently stopped to look at the marquee.

When I recalled this event as a youngster, my entire family said that we were never in Seattle.

When I was growing up, Aunt Sheila came to Los Angeles for a visit and confirmed the event, much to the surprise of my family.

My reason for saying this is to remind us to be careful of what we say in front of infants as it may affect their lives. This seems farfetched, but if I remembered as an infant, so could others.

Being Alone

At about the age of three, I was lonely and felt ignored. So, I hid on the running board of our old automobile as my father and mother drove away. I held onto the door handle for support. They drove for quite a distance. Much to their surprise, when they stopped the car at an intersection, I stood up. They asked me why I had done this. I said, "I was lonesome and wanted attention." They hugged and kissed me and drove me back home. Their presence made me happy.

The Flu Epidemic (1914)

I remember my uncle "Max" going into each home on our street to bring food, especially oranges, to the sick during the 1914 "flu epidemic." Big red-lettered signs were tacked onto the front porch of the houses saying "Quarantine." He would bathe and feed the ill to attempt to reduce their fevers, without regard for his own health. I asked him why he did it as the disease was so contagious. He said, "They would probably die if I didn't take care of them." Some actually survived because of his magnanimous love of humanity.

I, as a child, would wonder why GOD allows people to die in such a terrible manner.

Illness

When I was four years old, I had seizures and commented, "The sky is getting skinnier." I recall repeating this numerous times, but the family ignored me, probably dismissing this as child prattle. It wasn't until I was considerably older that these seizures were diagnosed as "petit mal." Fortunately, the drug Dilantin was prescribed as a treatment with success. (I am one of the oldest patients using this drug for that many years with minimum side effects.)

Norfolk Street (*1917*)

I was with my family in New York for the third time at the age of six. My father's business kept him away from home for months at a time while my mother, Sadie, stayed at her brother's apartment in the Bronx.

My two older sisters, Anne and Dot, and I lived with our grandparents in an apartment building at the corner of Norfolk Street and Delancey. We slept in a room that overlooked busy Norfolk Street with the pushcarts and filth that accompanied them. Horse manure was everywhere.

The apartment was on the sixth floor. It had a staircase and a fire escape for its exit. We had gaslight, as Edison had not yet invented the electric bulb. The toilet was in the basement.

My grandparents slept in the only bedroom, which was at the rear of the apartment. They kept a chamber pot under the bed for accommodation.

At night my sisters Anne and Dot used the only furniture in the front room, a chair and a rocker to sleep on. They would argue as to who would get the chair. I had to learn to sleep while semi-standing in a corner of the room, supported by spreading my elbows apart. Needless to say, many falls were a part of the scheme.

"C'est la guerre."

School

In the morning I walked to school through all the debris, ice, snow, and horse manure. It was a very cold, smelly winter.

I attended class with chattering teeth as the temperature was below zero. The school had no heating system, and I had only minimal clothing to wear.

Norfolk Street 2001

The teacher told us stories as we huddled together for warmth. Recess sent us out of doors to play in the snow. We slid and threw snowballs with frozen hands. It was an experience I will never forget.

I had to find my way home alone; I am sure I was often lost, but I eventually found Norfolk Street and the old brick building where we lived. I remember one day my two older sisters were standing on a corner and crying because they were so cold. They had very little clothing. We were very poor. My mother came and fed us in our meager quarters. All we had was a coal stove for heat.

Why we were there, I will never know.

Further Illness (*1924*)

At an early age, I had paroxysmal tachycardia from time to time without exertion. When I was thirteen years of age, my Aunt Anne Feinfeld took me to the senior doctor at the Board of Health in Los Angeles.

After he examined me, he stated that I had a bad heart. I told him, "I want to live long enough to be able to vote at least once." He said, "You will probably die within a year."

I was strong willed and determined to live. I decided to build up my body. I purchased a five-strand pull-apart elastic exerciser. I started with one strand and eventually increased to five. I went to the beach and watched the strong men in action. I was much smaller than they, yet I learned to stretch the five strands with ease.

Note: I vowed that if I survived, I would never miss an election. I voted every time, even once by mail while in the hospital for an appendectomy.

I am happy that the examining physician was not aware that paroxysmal tachycardia is a functional condition and not an organic disease.

The Appendectomy (*1931*)

While taking my junior final examination in medical school, I developed an acute right abdominal pain.

I was hospitalized immediately. The teaching surgeon did an emergency appendectomy.

Years later, I again had lower-right abdominal pain. An X ray revealed that my appendix was still in its original position.

What a surgeon!!! What did he resect?

Football
(An Episode, 1932)

I was a senior medical student and served as the Assistant Doctor for the Fremont High School football team. The physician in charge felt I was qualified to treat the injured football players.

The team captain, John D., was the star. He was an extrovert and very handsome with a great ego. He never seemed to get enough accolades and hoorahs and often on contact with an opposing player would feign injury. When enough screaming and clapping from the fans brought him to his feet, he would insist on returning to play. I recognized this emotional behavior and told him to get up whenever he faked injury.

In the last game of the season, he extended his straightened right arm to block an opponent. There was no contact, but the force of overexerting his muscular arm was so explosive that he actually ruptured several intercostal muscles in his right ribcage. He immediately fell to the ground in a state of shock as his pain was very intense.

The crowd saw that he had not made physical contact with his opponent, and they began to boo and hiss as they thought he was faking. He was carried away on a stretcher.

I yelled to the crowd that he was severely hurt and pointed to his chest, but no one believed me.

I guess GOD somehow evens things up.

Fremont High School won the game and became the champions for the first time in the new league. Mr. Rizzo, the principal, and coach J.C. sent me a letter praising my treatment of injuries that kept the players in good condition, which contributed to their winning the pennant.

I was given a trophy for a job well done.

Fifteen Cents
(1933)

A cent is the one hundredth part of a dollar, or a basic monetary unit; a coin:

Dr. Moisha Pilson was my early partner in the practice of medicine. This was the Depression era, and we were sitting in a small counter café across the street from our first office clinic, eating a fifteen-cent lunch consisting of three different foods.

A poor young disheveled man sitting on the next stool had just finished his lunch and stated that he was unable to pay for it. He remarked that he had not eaten in three days and felt faint.

Suddenly, the owner, boss, cook, dishwasher, and sweeper all in one yelled at this poor fellow, "I will beat you up if you do not pay for your lunch."

I leaned over and said to Moisha, "I have eight cents and if you have seven cents, he won't beat the boy up." He nodded his agreement.

After we paid for the boy's lunch and our own, we had no money left. The previously hungry one cried and thanked us for our generosity.

How sad to be so poor!

Thank GOD times have changed. Let us thank our government for the progress made.

A Flying Saucer
(Murrieta Hot Springs, 1937)

On a warm evening in July, my wife Ruth and I were walking on the resort's lovely grounds overlooking a relatively bare low hill. It was approximately thirty feet high. There were neither telephone poles nor wires visible. We were holding hands, enjoying the wonderful air, and commenting on how quiet and beautiful it was. Some of the people were in the clubhouse, and others were busy putting their children to bed.

When we reached the back of the grounds, we suddenly noticed a very quiet low flying saucer coming towards us over the mountain. It stopped about thirty or forty feet above and away from us. It had three or for low-caliber lights vertically spaced on either side of the cabin. A private ocean-going vessel of equal size would hold six to eight passengers. If there were people aboard, they would have been of small stature.

It hovered and slowly came toward us. We were transfixed and unable to speak. A tension came over us.

We felt we were in a controlled space vacuum and were unable to move. We thought we were going to be "sucked" aboard momentarily. The flying saucer stayed only seven to ten minutes. Suddenly, it reversed itself and backed away at great speed without any sound or smoke. Were we in shock? Yes. We had just been confronted by something from outer space!!!

Needless to say, our sleep was disturbed as we relived the event all night long. We had questions without answers. We could hardly wait until the next morning to go to see the area. There were no posts, telephone poles or wires, just a grassy hill with a low growth of weeds.

We asked a number of guests if they had seen the flying object, but no one had. The daily newspapers made no reference to the incident.

If we were abducted, we had no memory of it.

The Big Fight
(1942)

It so happened that over the years of hard work, sweat and tears, my father and I acquired a wrestling-boxing arena in San Bernardino, California. Sam was in the food concession business and so was able to sell his products to the fans.

One night there was to be a very good fight and the backer was selling tickets like mad. The arena had limited seating, and the board of health officer was always present at these events to make sure that we did not sell more tickets than we had seats.

Well, the promoter was selling tickets beyond capacity and I knew that the health officer present would close our arena. I went over to the promoter and said that he would have to return the excess ticket money. He argued with me and I was sure he was going to punch me, but I was very definite and said that the fights would not go on unless the money was refunded. Many disgruntled ex-pugs with their ladies were thus denied entrance.

Once the fighters were ready to begin, there was no doctor from the fight game there to check them out. He failed to show up that night.

The promoter came over to me and said in a very sweet voice, "We cannot go on with the fights without a doctor" and with I being a physician, he sheepishly begged me to check the fighters and be present for the bouts. The fly in the ointment was my not being approved by the State Athletic Commission. So he started calling Sacramento to have me approved as the attending physician. Fortunately, the commissioner was available to approve me so that the fights could go on.

I, being knowledgeable as to the character of the usual promoter in the fight game, demanded my fee in advance or I would not officiate. He said that he would pay me later. I said, "No, now." He reluctantly paid me and the fights went on. I told the promoter I had no trauma materials or oxygen, so if a fighter was seriously hurt, he would be sent immediately to the emergency hospital for attention and repairs.

Nevertheless, the bouts proved to be successful, but when the fighters went to the dressing room to shower and get paid, guess what? The promoter had disappeared with all the gate receipts!

The fighters said, "We will put out an alarm as to his character and evil deed. If he's ever found, it will be his demise."

Fire Aboard
(1945)

I was aboard a DC-3 airplane headed for New York to continue my training in the field of plastic surgery. Weather conditions were very stormy and the plane was bouncing about from the thrusts of the very strong winds.

A fellow passenger suddenly screamed, "The port engine is on fire." Passengers became frightened in disbelief. Many started saying their prayers and hugging each other in dismay. Their faces suddenly became strained and gaunt.

Over the loudspeaker came the captain's fears, "I have no means to douse the fire. We are up very high. Should the flames hit the gas tanks, it will be the end for us all. I will try to make a safe landing, but it may be too late. We are in the Lord's hands now."

Strained as I was, I quickly grabbed the movie camera I had brought with me to use at the convention. I started to film the anxious faces and burning engine. One of the male passengers supported me from falling as the plane was bouncing up and down and sideways.

We all felt that we were doomed and about to die. Why my mind went to preserve the event on film

I will never know. My hope was that if we perished, someone would find it. No one screamed and all huddled with bulging eyes and drawn faces.

The captain swerved the plane into a wet cloud, which miraculously extinguished the engine's flames. Inside, several people fell out of their seats and were injured. My camera also fell to the floor, opened, and over-exposed the film.

The captain spoke over the loudspeaker, which was still operable. He said, "The landing will be rough in this weather with just one engine for stabilization. GOD is with us through this horrible ordeal. The injured will be attended to on our arrival."

The landing was very rough but successful. All of the passengers and crew joined in giving three cheers for our wonderful captain. We all knelt and kissed the wet ground. The injured were carefully removed and taken to emergency.

Imagination, Fantasy, or Was It Real?

Imagination is the power of storing images in the memory or of recombining former experiences to create new images.

The incident I am about to relate occurred several days post-operative.

I was a patient in Cedars-Sinai Hospital for bypass cardiac surgery shortly after my dear wife Ruth died.

I was making a satisfactory recovery and alone in the ward. I was sitting up in bed with my feet exposed looking at the closed doors and walls around me.

Suddenly, my deceased wife floated through a closed door several beds away and put her hands up to her head to show me her new ultra-blond hair-do.

She looked so beautiful. I was hoping a nurse or doctor would come into the room and would see her so that they would believe what I saw. She walked over to my bed, put her two hands on my exposed feet, and suddenly disappeared.

I was alert and feeling at ease when this incident occurred.

I have never used hallucinating drugs. I swear it

really happened. Others have told me of similar experiences.

Only GOD can verify it.

Believe It or Not
(1998)

Stephen S. Weiss Temple, Rosh Hashanah.

My son, Sanford M. Gage, was aware of the incident I am about to describe.

We were seated in the temple when a fly came and set itself upon my right wrist. I motioned to Sandy to observe this. He suggested I shush it away. I replied, "I've tried several times and it keeps returning."

As the sermon progressed, this fly did not leave. I moved my arm to swish the fly away, but it immediately returned. This went on the entire time of the service, which lasted three hours. Just as it ended, the fly flew away.

I felt that my deceased wife Ruth was with me the entire time and then returned to her resting place. A very unusual experience!

What do you, the reader, think?

Panic Avoided
(Royce Hall Thirtieth Anniversary Season)

I was sitting in the Royce Hall Theatre, a packed house, with my oldest son Sanford. The wonderful chamber music was about to commence when the woman sitting next to me said to her husband, "I smell something and it is frightening me. I think that there is something wrong with the air conditioning."

Her fear was mounting and I, a physician, recognized and sensed a person with fear of being in a crowded area, which is called "claustrophobia."

I have always been blessed with a good sense of smell and did not notice any odorous cause of her complaint.

I leaned over and said, "I'm sorry, lady, I went to a new barber, and he shampooed my hair and put something on it and the smell is awful."

She was becoming panic stricken, complaining about the bad odors with fear in her voice. If not controlled, she could have caused a riot with potential injuries and death.

The orchestra leader turned his head and motioned for us to quiet down. People were saying, "Hush, hush."

She asked me again, "Are you sure you are telling me the truth?" I informed her that there was no cause for alarm.

I held her cold, clammy hands until they warmed.

I never told her the truth about my invented barber story.

A Monarch

I was playing golf at the Van Nuys golf course with the singles group, fifty and older, of which I am a member. They were yakking, swinging, bubbling over with continuous conversation, an effervescent group.

A monarch butterfly soared about. Each one of our foursome hit a ball ahead of me. Just as I was about to tee off, the same butterfly flew down and sat on my Tee. It seemed to have an injured wing. I swished it, but I could not get it to leave. The players and I seemed to become transfixed in its presence.

It was a strange but wonderful feeling. I felt my wife's presence. The butterfly reacted by moving its injured wing in response.

It seemed a long interval but must have been only a couple of minutes. The butterfly seemed to respond to me only. It suddenly lifted up in a lovely whirl and flew away. I then regained my composure and hit a fine golf shot.

The other contestants did not rush me to hit the ball as they usually do, not to chase the butterfly away. They must have been transfixed as I was. They said, "What a beautiful monarch!"

Arnold Palmer, a golfing legend, lost his loving father just before he embarked on his wonderful professional golfing career. The day he started play, he looked up at a beautiful rainbow and said he "knew his father was up there watching him."

Whatever this means!

Memories

I remember taking the train from Los Angeles to New York. It seemed forever, as I was just three.

I had been there when the 1933 earthquake shook down parts of our walls. The fireplace landed on our sofa. What a mess!

I was present at our first blackout at 10:00 P.M. Sirens were screaming. We were bowling as a team, and I had three strikes in my first game when the lights went out. We huddled together in fright. We went outside and saw large unrecognizable aircraft flying very high. We thought we were going to be attacked. I will never know if my first three hundred game was spoiled by the interruption.

I heard Paderewski play the violin. I was just ten. I did not realize how great he was until I was older and understood his talent compared to others.

I was there when our overloaded deep sea fishing boat became stranded on a submerged rock bed. Panic followed as water started to break through the hull.

Many of us climbed off the boat and onto the slippery rocks to push the boat back onto the sea. The holes in the hull were immediately covered with plastic sheeting. We continued a slow, frightening pace with a listing ship. There were a few casualties.

The captain was devastated and apologized to the patrons.

I was there when Mary, a friend, won the lottery. It was a great time for her, as she was a student with minimal funds.

I was there when the airplane's port engine caught fire. The captain said we would probably crash. Luckily, we landed in one piece.

I was there when each of my children and their children graduated with honors. Congratulations!

I was there when my great-grandson Benjamin was born. What a thrill to see him take his first breath!

Each individual must progress in life so that recounting events becomes a form of entertainment rich in excitement and pride.

Ruth's Joke

You know you are old when everything hurts. What doesn't hurt, you do not have!

The ladder of life is full of splinters. But they always prick the hardest when we're sliding down!

Guy on a first date. A friend fixes him up with a girl and says, "Go and get candy and perfume."

He goes to the drugstore and gets the items, and the pharmacists says, "Don't you want some rubbers?"

"Oh, no," he replied. "If it rains, I'm not going."

Lady goes to the pet store and sees a frog throwing kisses at her. She buys the frog, sets him on the passenger seat while driving home, and it keeps trying to kiss her. She gives in and the frog turns into a prince. What does she do? She turns into the next motel!

Ruth's Saying

When love and skill work together, expect a miracle.

Always remember to forget the trouble that passed away, but never forget to remember the blessings that come each day.

When GOD created man, She was only joking!

Ruth's Lunchbag Notes to Sol

For all the times I don't say the things I should,
I thank you for all the times you understood
Love ya.
Me

You are a part of me I could never live without—
and I hope and pray I never have to!

Let me be the person that you walk with in the
      mountains
Let me be the person that you pick flowers with
Let me be the person that you tell all your inner
      feelings to
Let me be the person that you turn to in sadness
Let me be the person that you smile with in
      happiness
Let me be the person that you love.
Love ya.
Me

Age is a quality of mind
If you have left dreams behind
If hope is lost
If you no longer look ahead
If your ambitions are dead

You are old
But if from life you take the best
If in life you keep the zest
If love you hold
No matter how the years go
No matter how the birthdays fly—you are not
old!

Dr. Sol Goldberg's Jokes
(For a very funny old-age)

Note: These jokes came to me in the middle of the night and I thought that they were so funny that you might enjoy one of my silly moods.

People say, "It's so nice to get old." Just wait and see and you will find out for yourself!

The doorway is never wide enough as I often bump one hip or the other when passing through even though I am not fat.

The spasms in my feet let me know I'm alive with electric stimuli. Sometimes my tears just flow.

The wrinkles in my drooping face have people asking me why I always look angry.

The tremor in my hand sometimes spills the coffee on my clean shirt and pants. They tell me not to drink coffee. Do I tell them what to drink?

The untied shoelace allows my shoe to fall off. I almost trip.

I just finished urinating and I have to go again. My clock needs fixing.

I read the newspaper with a magnifying glass. The sentence seems so long that I forget what I read at the beginning and why I read it in the first place.

I am still able to drive, and when I get there, I do not always remember why I went.

Children have no patience with me, but I still love them.

They say laughs are good for the soul—What do I have to laugh about?

I used to be able to run like a deer—now I am able to walk like a turtle.

When a comic tells a joke, I can't tell it's over until I hear the people howl and applaud. I act like I heard the punch line and smile.

I take out my bottle of pills and then I'm not sure if I took them. So, I call my doctor and ask him if I took them. He asks, "How should I know?"

What kind of a doctor is he if he doesn't know?

When I go to the movie theater, I often fall asleep and then they turn on the bright lights, which wake me up. The usher asks me to leave, as the new show will start after they clean up. The manager won't give me my money back even though I didn't see the movie. Is that fair?

Our Son Terry M. Goldberg, Esq.

Background:
Lived at home.
Was a good student and excellent mechanic.
Could fix and repair everything and anything.
Built an athlete's body through weight lifting.
Went to college and became an attorney of note.
He married young and had three smart children.
Divorced and remarried: hard worker.

His advice:
Teach children to stand on their own two feet.
Teach independence for security reasons.
Set limits on children's behavior and study
    habits.
Make them feel secure.
Maintain a budget and express limits.
A child has no experience, so the adult MUST
    teach.

Essays

Arkansas Tornadoes
(April 1998)

Winds at two hundred and fifty
to three hundred miles per hour in Arkansas.
Are we listening or is it not our problem?
Maybe it is just news.
Twisters rip.
Thirty-two killed in Atlanta, thirty in Jefferson.
Five more tornadoes hit the day before Easter.
One of the worst disasters ever.
With so many homes destroyed.
Devastation enormous.
One tornado was one half to one mile wide and
      three
miles long. How terrible!
Is this GOD's wrath on man's misbehavior?
Vice president (at the time) Al Gore was
      immediately
flown to the site to assist.

How nice!

43

Bombs in Colorado

April 29, 1999. Two armed youths clad in dark ski masks and Mafia trench coats killed eleven individuals in an apparent suicide and created a massive crime scene at the school in Littleton, Colorado. They used many weapons including booby traps, high-powered rifles, guns, and tossed pipe bombs into a crowd of terrified innocent students.

Our president and the entire world were profoundly shocked at the terrible tragedy of wanton loss of young lives. It appeared to be a carefully planned turmoil of death.

Children must be taught and watched so any deviation from normal behavior may be rectified before the growth of hatred and destruction develop.

Our prayers go out to the family and friends in their grief.

Note: This can occur in any community including yours and mine regardless of race, creed, or color.

An Episode I Witnessed

As I was about to leave a shopping center in the Marina Del Rey area, I saw an unkempt, odd-looking male in his forties, in stained shorts and a very wrinkled T-shirt. His boots were badly run down at the heels.

A slow-moving automobile leaving a parking place was about to pass this stranger when he suddenly lurched into the side of the automobile, groaned, and then lay motionless on the pavement.

A woman screamed and the moving automobile came to an abrupt halt. People gathered around to help the injured man, but he showed no response. Paramedics were called and soon arrived with their sirens screaming.

I had witnessed the entire event and was at the man's side. As a physician, I knew the man was a fake. Just as the ambulance attendants were scurrying to the "injured" man's care, I yelled, "There's a rat!" The man jumped up in fright and ran away.

The ambulance driver and attendants thanked me and then disappeared on call to a genuine injury.
Note: This is a true story. Insurance companies are often defrauded in just this manner.

Failings

A fault or natural weakness:

A List of Man's Failings:

1. Closing of the Savings and Loans by mismanagement, personal greed, or even theft. Is man out of control?
2. Is the disease AIDS here to repress man's desires and promiscuity?
3. Are wars necessary, or are they for profit and personal gain?
4. Are fires started for destruction of property in anger or for pleasure and excitement without regard for human lives?
5. Drugs, whether pure or not, are sold by pushers for profit?
6. Was the excessive beating of Rodney King for personal pleasure by bigoted officers warranted?
7. Public officials may direct funds for their own personal use often by vicarious means.
8. Automobile accidents create more horrendous trauma due to excessive speeding.
9. Earthquakes and floods cause devastation

and loss of lives. Is this GOD's release of tensions? He sure must have many.

10. Does inflation create greater profits for only some?

11. Should smog created by man be allowed without regard for the health of humanity?

12. Forests are being destroyed or reduced for personal gain without regard for the effects on our planet.

13. The well-publicized trial of O.J. Simpson left many questions unanswered.

14. Is GOD trying to tell us something? Man should listen.

They say, "You cannot take it with you."

You sure can. Your records of deeds on this earth are yours and only yours.

To Mr. "Bill" Clinton

A thanks
from the people of our blessed
United States of America
and all the nations of this wonderful world of
      ours.

When a job had to be done,
who was there?

Mr. "Bill" Clinton.

When warring nations decided to act,
Who stopped them short?

Mr. "Bill" Clinton.

When troubles started at home,
who halted them in their tracks?

Mr. "Bill" Clinton.

A world,
jealous of our wealth and prosperity,
would love to have you for their leader.

When you were threatened with impeachment,
you responded with strength and courage
for your country's welfare.

The best peacetime prosperity.
The least unemployment in our history,
with minimum inflation.

What else can one say?
Our hats are off to you, "Sir."

It is too bad that the Constitution
does not allow a third term in office
or you would triumph.

We thank you,
Mr. "Bill" Clinton

The United States of America
and yes,
the entire world.

Mother Teresa, Nun

"A saint in the form of a human being."

I would be remiss if I didn't relate my feelings toward this wonderful "Angel" of our times.

Her life was devoted to the sick, the poor, and the disadvanaged. She ministered to millions of people in India. If one were ill, starving, and even dying, to be received by this wonderful lady must have been an experience to the receiver as being attended to by an angel.

She administered to millions in her frail, bent, bony body fraught with multiple ills. It never stopped her from delivering consolation and aid to the populace.

She founded a convent for the impoverished, the needy, and the maimed. She traveled extensively to raise money for her humanitarian deeds. She was awarded the Nobel Peace Prize, which she so justly deserved.

The wrinkles in her beautiful face with her wonderful smile only gave more confidence to the needy. GOD must have wanted her in heaven, but HE waited eighty-seven years for her return.

Secretary-General Javier Perez de Cuellar said "She is peace in the world." What an epitaph!

President Clinton remarked that she was an incredible person, and he rewarded her with the Congressional Gold Medal of Honor.

She was labeled "Saint of the gutters." A tribute she so genuinely deserved.

One gives and one receives. "Teresa gave and she received."

Making her a "Saint" is little more praise for her.

She received the highest rewards in return for her deeds in the eyes of a person in need, or the touch from a suffering soul and the dying. She asked so little and received so much. An angel must have flown over her in envy all her life.

The world is certainly a better place because of her deeds and presence.

Now GOD will enjoy her presence with the same love that the world enjoyed with her understanding that meant so much.

We wish she could have lived on earth forever, but her deeds and actions will not be forgotten.

A simple approach with a grandiose result for simply giving of one's self was her reward.

GOD only allows one super being such as "She" every millennium. The world could use one much more often.

Her clasped hands with bony fingers extending gave faith and support to so, so many.

Her smiles were breathtaking, as though from an angel at peace.

Hug

I remember as a small child trying to do the impossible. I would climb too high or jump too far and fall. My crying would bring a hug from my mother, Sadie.

The comforting sensation made me curious to test others on hugging as to their reactions in various conditions.

When I was a young physician, at the Los Angeles County General Hospital in the Depression era, I would often hug the terminally ill indigents, male and female alike. Tears came unabatedly as I felt so helpless, especially when they asked me not to leave them.

Responses to My Survey on "HUG"

A blind elderly lady:
"I feel a closeness and friendship. You're wonderful.

I wanted that hug. I get it so rarely."

A recent widower: "A feeling of support while grieving."

A widow: "I feel warm—tenderness, I'm so sad and alone."

Responses from Couples

F: "That hug was wonderful—
I feel that I'm flying to another planet."
M: "I feel big-warm-awkward—I needed it."

F: "Having some fun!"
M: "Felt sad and horny."

F: "Feels very good. Everyone should have a hug."
M: "Feeling of security . . . eliminates loneliness."

F: "I don't want to let go."
M: "I do not feel alone now."

F: "A hug starts the tears rolling.
What a way to cleanse the eyes without drugs."
M: "It arouses my whole body to love.
I feel important."

> Two hospitalized patients:
> One said, "What a simple form of therapy!
> All painful symptoms disappeared."
> The other said, "A hug makes me devilish.
> I feel stronger."
> Two women meet at a restaurant and hug:
> One said, "Warm, cuddly. Happy."
> The other said, "A heart warming, priceless treasure."

Two priests at a church meeting—hugged.

Father A: "Sincere blessings from the Almighty."
Father B: "A righteous place for man to live in peace with GOD."

Two rabbis in their conventional robes and from opposite sides of the pulpit met and hugged. I immediately asked their response.

Rabbi A: "I felt security and the presence of GOD."
Rabbi B: "I had a feeling of love, excitement, and the presence of GOD."

Note: Both priests and rabbis referred to GOD.

Tiger Woods, the greatest young golfer, after winning each tournament hugs his caddie and his original teacher-father.

In the prize ring, the fighters after pummeling each other for a number of rounds "hug" each other in a spirit of bravado.

Katja Seizinger and her German team rejoiced on the mountainside hugging each other after receiving her second gold medal.

When Mark McGwire hit sixty-two home runs, he went around and hugged everybody.

A male Navajo stated he experienced "a high feeling of warmth and intensity." I asked if he would hug a male. He shouted: "Men do not hug; it is repulsive!"

I quickly left with my scalp.

A king or a queen, a billionaire or even a Pope cannot have greater depth of feelings than the lowliest person on earth, with just a simple hug, the feelings are GOD's gift to man.

My Conclusion

A simple hug is comforting, pleasant, and says, "I forgive and love." It says it all faster than a speeding bullet and works better than any drugs without ill effects.

Guns

I believe guns should be outlawed. They are not only used for protection; they are mostly used for destruction by criminals and often by crazed or psychotic individuals.

The Constitution of the United States, Appendix C, "The Bill of Rights," enacted December 15, 1791, Article II: "A well-regulated militia, being necessary to the security of the free state, the right of the people to keep and bear arms shall not be infringed."

Times have changed. The Constitution, written more than two hundred years ago, does not protect man today. Firearms are used by angry, sick, illiterate, or disgruntled individuals and mobs bent on destruction against their fellow man.

I say again, "Change the Constitution to outlaw guns except for the militia that protects the citizens of the United States of America."

Headlines are a constant reminder of the dangers of guns to the populace with daily incidents about death and injuries to innocent victims.

A young man jumped up on a table and opened fire, calmly spraying bullets across the room until three students wrestled him to the ground. Two deaths followed with multiple injuries to twenty-two students.

Ask Beverly Oliver from Jonestown how she felt when she said, "I lost all I had, which is my boys."

Today, a rider shot and killed a bus driver and himself. The bus careened off a bridge onto an apartment house. It is the worst bus accident in the history of the city of Seattle. People scrambled to help. This could have been avoided if guns were no longer available.

If the previous stories are not enough, today in the twenty-first century, a six-year-old shot and killed another six-year-old student.

More unnecessary injuries and deaths will occur if guns are permitted and available.

How nice—in a "sane America," no one listens and guns are available not only for protection but for destruction.

We occasionally read about disgruntled employees who shoot their company's executives, which can certainly destroy any business.

Give it some thought, Americans. You could be the next innocent victim. We must repeal the Second Amendment of the Constitution of the United States of America for our safety.

Records state that one hundred officers were shot in the line of duty in Los Angeles in 2000. There is no more to be said. Only action is the answer.

President Clinton was asking Congress for two hundred and eighty million dollars for gun control.

As a physician: I can only see destruction with

the legality of guns. If you had seen the helpless, hopeless cases I saw in the hospital and those in the morgue, you would undoubtedly agree with me.

The Pampered Child

- I don't care for anything.
- I am mad about my age, my friends, and even my enemies if I have any.
- Life has been hard since my first cry to survive.
- Is this a fun ride on earth?
- What do I have to do to be happy?

Gosh, when I was a real young kid, I was told what to wear, to clean up my room, to throw out the garbage, to make the bed, to take the dog a bone, and to eat my breakfast.

I sure am mad that the grammar school teacher wouldn't let me pull the girl's hair in front of me. She had a funny face with freckles and would wince when I came close to her. I didn't know if she liked me or not. I never kicked her but thought it would be fun to hear her scream.

What is wrong if I threw my bag from my lunch on the playground? It only flew away and the principal scolded me for it. She made me pick up papers I never threw.

What's wrong if I pull the tail of the scroungy brown dog from up the street? No one plays with him, only me. I think he likes me. That is how I play.

No one pays attention to me, so I throw torn papers on the neighbor's lawn. That is the only time the old crab ever talks to me. No one else does except to scold.

I am the best reader in my class, and the teacher won't let me read as she says I talk too much. I could talk a lot more, but she won't let me read.

When my mom picks me up, she asks if I behaved. I said, "The teacher is mean to me, and just 'cause the girl in the desk in front of me doesn't do good, I am to blame as I talk too loud and she says she cannot hear the teacher's questions."

When I am in class, I think of how hard my dad works and how hard my mom cleans. They almost never talk to me except to scold when I interrupt them when they are talking. How else will they hear me if I am not permitted to talk? So, sometimes I scream and then they spank me for no good reason and I am put to bed without the rest of my dinner and then later they both come by and sing a lullaby with the lousiest of voices. I try to hold my ears. They then kiss me "goodnight," and I fall into a dream of beautiful birds floating in the sky and wish that I were one.

Injuries

One never thinks it will apply to them.
Only others fall.

Fractures are common in this world of ours. Trauma creates a sudden change of our activities. Pain and swelling become activated in an attempt to try to heal the site.

Before, we were free to walk, move on our own, or drive without restrictions. Now we no longer can.

If we are lucky, we will have someone to help us until we can once again do our thing.

If we are unlucky and have no one to aid us, our plight is extremely difficult.

To propel alone with grave injuries, is "hell on earth." Each painful movement adds to the original trauma. Casts for fixation and possible surgical correction may be necessary.

The best advice is to say to yourself, "in due time, I will look back on this trial period as another episode in my life. I may be stronger emotionally as a result of this."

So, look forward to a better day.

a—"Word"

Adventure

A bold undertaking that involves some risk or excitement. A remarkable experience; to dare or venture:

You can have an adventure right at home in your own neighborhood. All it takes is a little effort to find out what activities and meetings are available where you live.

Do not act aloof or put up a barrier so you will not be disappointed. Being friendly and a smile will bring a reward. Tensions will disappear and you will enjoy a gratifying experience. The thrill of associating with people will bring new friends.

Some of their tales may be dull and others exciting, but your time will be wisely spent. It is true that most of us are timid and not always sure of ourselves, but meeting new people can create lasting friendships.

Call it adventure.

Beautiful

Today is a beautiful day!
The sun is shining.
Birds are soaring and singing for mates.
Automobiles are tooting and speeding by.
Everything seems to be in motion.
My head is swirling and I feel like whistling.
Is there something in the air?

Did I sleep better last night?
Did I eat the right foods?
Have I lost or gained weight?
What can it be?

I finally made a decision after weeks and months
      of
turmoil what to do with the rest of my life.
Just making the decision,
hopefully, it is the right one,
I can now think clearly with my mind at ease.

See the birds in the sky.
Feel the wind on my cheeks.
Now I shall pursue my goal in life
when excitement with growth is the theme of the
      times.

So, just do it.
The rewards will be aplenty.

Believe

To accept as true or real, to credit with veracity;
to have confidence in and to trust:

One must have a dream and then proceed with
    the
supposition of success.
If the subject or object seems impossible, there is
nothing wrong in trying to do the impossible.
If it is a dream, then go for it even though the
    odds are
gigantic.

You must believe in yourself.
If you don't, you will try many things without
    assurance
and have a meaningless existence.
If you do, you will accomplish more on this earth
    so
that you as well as others may benefit from your
    talents
and efforts.

You will be happier, more thoughtful, well
    received,
and by so doing, you will be rewarded and will
    feel
good about yourself.

In addition
how nice it will be for you
to add some humor along the way,
which will add spice to your life.

This will spread to others
so they will also benefit from it.

Once you accomplish your goal,
seek another and yet another
and life will be a challenge with many delightful
results.

You can create,
develop to your capacity and beyond
and be proud of your existence.

Believe that you can jump over the moon
and maybe you can in your dreams.

The impossible has brought man:

>Life
>the world
>the Sun
>the Moon and a vessel to get there
>an astronaut to hit a ball with a golf club
>for all to see on television
>in our own home,
>the radio
>the computer
>the Internet
>what next?

So believe in yourself
and try a difficult project,
which is success in itself and perchance
you will do the impossible.

Challenge

A summons to fight, an exception taken;
to defy; to object to:

Life is one long challenge.

A newborn infant cries to survive.
It is also a form of communication.

This is the way a baby commands attention
and is heard.

As a youngster, you scream and push
and even shove to get attention.

Some bite, spit, or have tantrums
as a means of getting heard.

Children run, jump, or throw a ball,
anything for expression of feelings.

Then along comes school
to learn, develop the mind,
compete and improve one's skills.

Later, it is pimple time.
It is not funny; squeezing them is some relief and
        is
something to do.

A new experience, sex—is now an important part
        of life
with fears and lack of confidence.

What to do with one's life?

How to prepare?

There are always new fields to conquer.

Whether to go to college, to get a degree,

What field to follow?

Life is one continuous challenge.

You have to meet it head on or it will be wasted.

That is your responsibility.

Crying

To utter a loud shrill; joy; fear; surprise; to
    clamor;
to weep; to shout; to proclaim; or even to scream:

So many different meanings.

The impoverished would be crying for food and
shelter, which often man does not choose to hear. If
he does, it is usually on a minimal basis and for a limited time, how unfortunate!

It is true: we cannot help everyone in the world.

Does GOD listen to all the people who have a le-
gitimate reason to cry? It is too vast a problem. Much
more crying than laughter exists.

Does the widow or widower have the right to cry,
and for how long? Some never stop.

It is a new experience to be alone.

People you knew as a couple tend to disappear.

The grieving individual is now placed in a new
environment and is usually along in years and often
in poor health.

It is very difficult to adjust to loneliness. A new
lifestyle is thrust upon you.

Crying seems to give some solace, but one has to

limit the frequency as well as length or it will over-whelm you.

You must start early to make a new life for yourself or you will be doomed to disaster.

Join a singles group with similar interests, and life can still be rewarding and exciting. It is much healthier than solitude.

Make new friends, see new places, and try new things. It will take you through this difficult period.
—GOOD LUCK WILL FOLLOW YOU—

Dear God

A being of supernatural powers; Believed in and worshiped; the omnipotent:

GOD, I am taking this liberty to ask you a few questions that may answer some of my doubts.

If you had one life to live, as we apparently have, would you choose to be:
A human being?
Male or female?
Or would you rather be a bird or a fish?

If you choose being human, would you want to be
a
doctor or a non-professional?

Would you want to be rich or poor
to see how it feels?

Would you rather not work
and be cared for and by whom?

Would you want to feel pain, love, hate, hunger,
or would you want to eliminate it?

Would you want to have wars, famine, crime,
or prevent them?

Would you want to be
a prima donna
a tyrant
a lover
or just one of the people?

Would you want everybody to be the same and
    equal?
Would you want to live without pain and
    suffering?
Would you want to live forever in ecstasy?

Wouldn't it be nice after you experienced some of
    our
problems if you could just eliminate them and
    create the
ideal world?

Have you thought about some of the problems
        that humans
face and wish they could be avoided?

Would you pray, and to whom?
GOD, I wish to apologize for taking the liberty to
        ask
some questions that maybe you can answer.

You see, my wife died recently and I miss her.

Difficult

Hard to do, achieve, or comprehend; not easy; hard to manage or satisfy:

So many things in life are difficult.

When one loses a mate of many years, almost every situation becomes a difficult problem. Discussions and reveries are a thing of the past.

Being alone, the nights are so long. Suggestions and even advice from well-meaning friends or relatives are difficult to accept.

One flounders and now simple tasks become confusing and frustrating. Our own judgment is questioned.

Shall the remaining spouse stay, move, retire, travel, look for a new spouse, cry, pretend they are now happy or even happier? It becomes a difficult period in one's life.

Only the remaining spouse knows one's inner true feelings.

Sleepless nights are now a part of one's lifestyle. Looking and feeling for an absent mate is a new experience and difficult to accept.

One asks GOD for help that one cannot always find.

You must and do go on with your life.

Hope

To desire something with some confidence of fulfillment.

After a severe illness or major surgery, a person feels it is an endless road to recovery. It will never come to pass. The patient is so overwhelmed with many examinations and procedures that any progress seems minimal. Waiting for results of tests really tries one's emotions.

One must follow doctor's orders. Every turn and movement requires a nurse to assist the early post-operative patient.

As your body shrinks away and you look in the mirror, it is with disbelief that you are that individual. You are told that you are doing well. You wonder, "Who are they looking at?" Encouragement is one part of their repertoire. Nevertheless, some improvement begins to occur.

To look to the future and wonder how you will eventually be is paramount in one's mind. The future has not yet told me how I will ultimately be.

Hope is my only weapon.

Life

The animate existence of an individual; a living
    being:

Man survives at the onset by being spanked until
    he
cries. This must be GOD's way of saying,
"Each must obey my rules for the privilege of
    life."

How we utilize our time is up to us.

We can waste it or grow and develop,
explore new areas and be constantly stimulated.

There are adventures for everyone.
Each new challenge is a stepping-stone
for learning and development.

Your life can be a gain or a loss.

Each individual has something to contribute.

"Can't" should not be a part of one's thoughts.
"Can" is only a three-letter word and is
    preferable.

Growth and excitement are here
for the industrious and inquisitive.

Try new challenges to stimulate one's interest.
You will be well rewarded.

Loss

Unable to find; mislay; unable to keep; to be
    deprived of:

There is an expression
"One man's loss is another man's gain."

This is not always true,
as in the loss of a loving mate.

Then there is no chance of recovery
and the loss remains permanent.

Tears keep streaming.

At times, you feel strong and can stand the shock.
Other times, you whimper and cannot
        comprehend.

Morning, noon, and night,
the loss is never recovered.

Without one's wonderful mate,
living is difficult.

How silly?
Crying is of no avail, but can one stop?

Memories are so vivid.
You try to recall the past.

Try as you might,
You cannot see your lost mate.

There is an abrupt lifestyle change.

You may seek the services of a psychiatrist.
You spill your guts with floods of tears.
You leave drenched and exhausted.

Jokes do not seem so funny.

Sometimes you are annoyed
when once you would have laughed out loud.

Friends you knew tend to disappear.

You are and feel alone.

You must make the choice to start anew.

With difficulty,
You must now adapt to a new lifestyle.

It is up to you.

"Go to it."

Pond

A body of water smaller than a lake; artificial or natural:

That is the dictionary definition. Mine is much different and has much more meaning to me.

We begin life in a small "pond" that consists of embryonic fluid within the uterus, our home for nine months.

The "pond" protects the fetus from harm and injury. "The "pond" increases in size to accommodate the growing fetus. To sustain life, it must and does maintain the proper pH (acid content).

The growing embryo takes on an awkward fetal position in the uterus as each system develops.

The only contact the embryo has with its new world is through the umbilical cord and the pond in which it moves, kicks, and swims as the various organs grow and develop to form the newborn.

The first response to life requires the intake of oxygen and the elimination of carbon dioxide for survival. The infant cries as it leaves its home, stating,

"I MADE IT!"

Proof-read

To read, copy, or a printer's proof against the original manuscript for corrections and improvements.

Just imagine if we could proofread our actions before we do them.

We are placed on this earth without previous knowledge; yet we have to make decisions as we go along. Many times we have to make monumental changes without any experience.

How is it possible to be correct each and every time?

As "children growing up," we are taught by parents or elders what is right or wrong. Sometimes the adults are not sure themselves. They often tend to direct your future work and sometimes marriage, not knowing your capacity to accept either lifestyle.

We have to make lifetime goal decisions as youngsters without knowing what the future has to offer.

Imagine a child saying "I want to be a doctor or a lawyer when I grow up." They certainly are not aware of what it entails.

We cannot proofread our future.

Should we marry?

A question we all ask ourselves. Life is full of anxieties and dilemmas.

If we could avoid errors, we could attain our greatest potential and be much happier with our existence.

Wonder

The dictionary states: that which arouses awe or admiration; a marvel; a feeling of puzzlement or doubt. To be filled with curiosity.

I wonder how a specific sperm fertilizes an egg and whoever thought up such an idea.

Where were you before you were born and why were you born?

Why honeysuckle smells sweet and why a lemon tastes sour?

Why birds fly and we cannot. A child often tries with a sickening thud.

When you look up in the sky and see the sun, the moon, and the stars, do you wonder who placed them there?

I wonder—is there really a GOD, an angel?

I wonder about life and death. Is there a heaven or a hell, an afterlife or is this it?

Why were we born, and for what purpose?

Does each of us have other lives?

Different sexes? Or is this it?

If so—for what reason?

I wonder why one should work so hard to accomplish a goal when the life span is so limited?

Would one put out more effort to become something if one knew that there was a future after the life we know?

Are we tested for something greater or worse depending on one's effort or behavior?

If we knew there was a better life for those who deserved it, would one try harder or would one not try if on this earth as we know it ends without a future?

"Wonder" is a magnificent word.

It's really a question without an answer—no wonder man is confused.

Did You Ever Think?

There might be a billion Earths?
There might be a billion GODs?
Whom would you talk or pray to or ask for
    advice?
Whom would you worship?

Of course this is far fetched. But, who knows what is beyond our earthly existence? Seers and philosophers have discussed human beings for centuries without knowledge or facts as to why we are here and also our future in heaven or hell if there is one.

I cannot ascribe to beliefs without proof; but I have a feeling that we are all here for a purpose. It does not seem right that we, the human race, are here for no good reason at all. So, I have to believe that each of us is born at this period in time and for a purpose.

Why try harder if there is no future?
Why accumulate knowledge and wealth?

There are a lot of **whys** without substance or knowledge. So, each one of us must make our own way according to our beliefs.

I feel there would be a great waste of energy that

each of us expends if there were no future in the school of life and the hereafter. That this world we know is final and that last before oblivion.

So, let us assume that there is a future and only one GOD and after our term on this earth, we graduate according to effort and accomplishments to another world for another school of higher education.

Well, enough philosophizing, because I have to see my first teacher in the kindergarten of life.

God Can Make a Tree!

Only GOD can make a tree;
You can bet!

HE made man with fingers to shake hands.

A tongue to say the truth and "thank you."
Even give a compliment when deserved.

Legs to do chores for oneself and others.

Eyes to see the sun, the moon and the stars
and human beings as decent people.

A nose to smell the flowers and a rat.

Ears to hear a baby's cry.

Fingers to touch the lips of your mate with love.

A brain to activate one's senses and organs.

Who else would think of a sperm piercing an egg
      for you and me?

Don't question HIM.
HE is smarter than you think.

The Nonbeliever

This is for the nonbeliever in GOD.

Did you ever create
      a bird that sings and flies,
      a horse that gallops,
      a rabbit with long ears,
      a camel with two humps,
      a fly that can walk on the ceiling?
Did you make man with a nose that can smell a
      rat?

Can you explain a good feeling
—eating or drinking something you like—
and even helping someone in need?

When your voice box opens up and you scream
      and
ask for help, isn't someone there for you?
Are you not heard?

Your skin rejuvenates to give you your beautiful
        tan.
Your eyes are for your vision to see beyond
        yourself.
Your ears are there to hear the cry of a newborn
and to listen to others in need.
You even have a larynx to tell tall tales.

Man is here to learn and to grow.
We are so lucky.
We are at a crucial period in time—the
        millennium—

How fortunate that we are now able to do our
        best for
humanity. It is our obligation for just being alive
        here
and now.

We are lucky to have had the privilege of the egg
and the sperm in a comfortable enclosure for our
        birth.

Be the best you can
so that you can hold your head up high.
When you meet your Maker,
be proud of your record on our Earth.

Think—
Did your feelings come without our Maker?

God Is So Good and At Times Seems So Cruel

I wonder why?

He gives and He takes;
He leaves a great void.

How terrible!

He deforms;
He makes great.

He develops hazards. . . .
for what purpose?

He creates life.

How wonderful!

Alone is often so bad;
Many of us have to suffer a loss.

Why?

As a couple,
You live a lifetime often struggling much of the
     way.

At the end, if you survive,
You may be alone.

How much suffering is enough?
The tears flow unabated at times.

We try to accept our plight, but with difficulty.

Is it fair after trying an entire lifetime
to be good, helpful, and to get ahead?

For what?

Tears flow again and again.

People say, "You are doing fine."
They can't feel the twangs in your heart.

Why should you?

GOD makes the rules—not you!

Hug loved ones when you can;
You can't when they are gone.

Why

This came to me in the middle of my sleep one
    night.

What does it mean?

Our specific sperm penetrated the ova to make
    you and me? What for?

Why are we here?
What is our role?

Why work so hard to develop and become
    something in
this wonderful world when we know—even with
    our
best efforts, this will all end?

Is this all there is?
Is there something else?

Is it all in vain?

Is there more in another life?
Are we in school to learn for another era?

What were we before?

Are we honed for a future better life closer to
    GOD?

Is it really over when we die?

We are not supposed to know.
Did man create a GOD for security reasons?
Or is there really one?

No human could make our world—
Only a GOD could.
Is HE experimenting to make the perfect world?

God

The Creator and Ruler of the universe, the
     Almighty.
Is HE or SHE real?

We as human beings decide if we believe in a
     GOD.
We should all know right from wrong.

Would you change your ways
if you were sure there is a GOD?
Would you cheat?
Would you lie?
Would you transgress?
Would you be more thoughtful, gracious,
Be on your best behavior at all times?

Are we here as in school to develop and grow?
Are we humans the privileged ones to have life?

When we meet our Maker,
We take our earthly record with us
as well as our previous thoughts and acts and as
     such, judged.
If we knew there is a GOD,
Would we live a different life so that
We could be rewarded for our efforts on earth?
Don't we all wish we really knew?

I want to believe there is a GOD and so I behave.
How about you?

God the "Creator"

Man believes he is so smart;
Many believe there is no GOD.

Who would have thought of an ovum and a sperm
to lay in a uterus for nine months
to fully form a baby?

A change of seasons
to allow the trees to bear fruit on a regular basis?

A way to keep the air clean?

Gave man the ability to think and create
    a toastmaster
    a shop to float on water
    a train to ride on tracks
    a robot
    an automobile
    a washing machine
    a radio
    a television set
    a voice to call for help or
    to say thank you for a kind act
    a computer (so I can write this book).

How great HE or SHE is?

What If???

Suddenly you could fly?
Change your sex at will?
Have more money than you could count?

Run faster than a deer?
Jump over the highest mountain?
Get a hole in one on every golf course?
Have intercourse nonstop?

Eat everything on the menu without gaining
    weight?
Would you enjoy your food more or maybe not at
    all?
Would you become more generous?

Your life would change for the better maybe?
Would you be happier?
Would you become philanthropic?
Perhaps you then would not look forward to
    anything?
Fail to progress?

Now—really become insecure?
What if you were born the opposite sex?
Would you taunt your sex?
Or would you like yourself as much?

Well, enough of what if.
You can dream as I have and have fun doing it.

93

Can you imagine what GOD went through
to create man?

I Wonder If Death as We Know It Is Final?

Is it just a change of bodily structure?

Will we see our family and friends in the hereafter?

Does it all cease here and now?

I don't believe it all ends here as I have had contact with my beloved deceased wife on several occasions.

When I speak to others who have lost someone dear, they informed me of similar experiences.

There must be another dimension one encounters where the lost one penetrates the ether and comes in contact with the earthly being. I would rather believe it is true than not.

It is more comforting to think that all our trials and tribulations on this earth are not "in vain" and there must be a future for us somewhere else.

Wherever that might be.

Good or Bad

You have the choice;
You can be good
Or you can be bad;
It is up to you!

If your choice is to be good,
You and others will benefit from your existence;
You will have a good feeling and be well
        rewarded
Regardless of responses from others;
Your life will be commendable.

If you decide to be bad,
Others will suffer and so will you.
Someday you will face your Maker.
Even if you try to hide your bad behavior,
You cannot.

Before GOD, your life is an open book.
You will have no answers and
You will suffer the consequences.

Our lives must be an experiment to learn
How to behave—

Do we belong in another existence?

So What?

What if the world were square?
Would we see others across the world in different
    countries at will?

What if the sky were yellow?
Would we have huge eyes or maybe only one eye?
It would be so bright.

What if trees grew downwards?
Would we see only roots and no branches?
If the trees grew downwards, so might the
    flowers.
Then we would never see their beauty.

What if water ran uphill?
Would we have trouble staying dry?

What if we knew what the other person was
    thinking?
Would we like them more or much less, as we
    would
know their true character?
They would have no privacy.

What if we were able to go into another
        dimension at
will? Would we get dizzy going back and forth?
Would we have dreams of other dimensions?

What if we lived for centuries?
Would we get bored with each other and become
hermits?

My Poetic Writings

A Dream Come True

Bouquets for Alan Shepard and John Glenn,
Astronauts and real American heroes,
Lifetimes of devotion and hard work,
Years of study with a dream
For you and me and the world.

"The First American in Space"—Alan Shepard.
Golf sure intrigued you.
You could not get a time to play at home.
So you played away on the moon to not lose your
    feel.
What a thrill!

"The First American in Orbit"—John Glenn
You circled Earth three times
And then—
Your triumphant return years later aboard the
    Shuttle
Did you go to look for Alan's lost golf ball?
No siree!
You went for the benefit of mankind,
To show that age is no barrier for success.
One can still fulfill one's dream—as you certainly
    did.

May GOD bless all astronauts;
We are indebted to YOU.
You are forever in our hearts,
True Americans.

When I Was Young

When I was young,
I could run like a deer.
I could eat or drink anything and digest it;
I could see everything and know what it meant.
I could remember where I was and what I did;
I could hit a nail right on the head with the
     smallest
hammer and hit the bull's-eye with an arrow at
     thirty paces.
I could get up on a horse and ride like a
     champion and
even dismount by myself;
I could read a poem and remember all the words
     and
repeat it at will—and even remember what it
     meant.
I could wish for the moon or the stars and find
     them;
I could try to be older and act like I knew more
     than I did.
I could hear a tune and recall and sing it.
I can look back and wish I had done more, and
     more,
and more.
How good to dream—it is for everyone, young and
     old.

I Wonder

I wonder. . . .
If I were born a cripple,
How would I feel?

I wonder. . . .
If I were born a different race and color,
what would be my reaction to man?

I wonder. . . .
if I were born gay or bisexual,
how would I react to life?

I wonder. . . .
if I were born the opposite sex,
how would I behave?

I wonder. . . .
if I were born a monarch or king,
how would I treat the populace?

I wonder. . . .
if I were a midget,
would I dislike people laughing at me?

I wonder. . . .
if I were a giant,
would I feel self-conscious or be proud of my size?

I wonder. . . .
if I had dyslexia,
how hard it would be to read?

I wonder. . . .
if there is an after or other life,
did I previously live in a different era?

I wonder. . . .
who thought of having the mountains and the
    seas,
    the stars and the sky
    the birds and the bees
    and yes, man?

I wonder . . . and I believe
there is a GOD.

I wouldn't want his job.

Am Me

"April 25th" is my birthday.
I can be alone or with a group.
I can love or hate,
I can or not be honest.
I can either grow, mentally developing with
     GOD's
help, or not.
I can love and please others all my life.
I can contribute for my privileges on this
     wonderful
planet, or not.
I can enjoy, carouse and kick my feet, and refuse
     to do
anything and deteriorate if I wish, or not.
I can produce for the benefit of mankind.
I can create a living being with my sperm and an
     egg.
How lucky I am!
I can lie and cheat and even inflict harm or be
     forthright
and honest.
I can either add to the quality of life for myself
     and for
others, or not.
I can feel, touch, laugh or cry as I wish.
I can be kind,
helpful to others or be selfish,
"for me only."

I can teach,
help the infirm, or not

I can contribute all my best offerings
during my stay on this wonderful planet Earth.

I thank GOD for all my privileges
and try to be the best I can.

That is how powerful I can be.
How lucky I am to have that choice and
     opportunity.

So be it.

Who

This word pertains to a child with a broken
　　home.

Whom do I live with?
Whom do I love?
Who loves me?

Whom do I hate?
Who hates me?

Who can I come to for advice?
Who will put me to bed at night?

Who will hold me when I am mad?
Who will laugh with me when I am glad?

Whom will I study with or ask for help when I
　　don't
know the answers?
Whom will teach me the facts of life?

You, my parents, should have thought about me,
before you had me.

Did you ever realize all the complications that
I will have as a result of your inability to get
　　along?

Parents—think of your children.

What a separation or divorce does to the child is
    inestimable.
Seek another avenue with understanding, before
    you
change your home life.

It could be so rewarding to you and your family.

Just give it one more chance.

Dreams

Dreams are here for everyone.

You can go to the sea.
You can go to the moon.
You name it.

From dreams come new ideas and progress.

You can climb the highest mountain.
Swim the deepest river
or never leave your abode.

Dreams are for reminiscing,
for growth
development
invention
for pleasure—how nice!

You can pretend that you are something or
     someone,
a bird or an airplane.
See how much fun it is to fly.
Be a fish or boat.
Swim or float on the water around the world.

Fantasies are there just for the asking.
Pretty nice, I would say.

This is a "God"-given prize.
Everyone can have as many as they like
without permission from anyone.

Make your own choices.

We can all have that same privilege,
young and old,
rich and poor alike.

You can be the greatest comedian,
star in your own film,
be a king or queen,
even a rabbit with long ears,
jump up and down just for fun.

Be a dog or a cat and be petted,
bark or meow just for merriment.

I like to dream.
I hope you do, too.

It seems like an amusement that everyone can
enjoy.

Predictions for the Great Millennium

Millennium Predictions
2009 and Beyond

The Millennium Philosopher's Predictions (With Tongue in Cheek)

I foresee and predict with sunglasses on good wishes for The Great Millennium.

New discoveries in the map of the human genome will add at least twenty-five years to one's life. New drugs will follow for a healthier society. More organ transplants will occur successfully without the enormous amount of drugs necessary to sustain their viability. Many current diseases will be only in the history books.

New methods for increased crop and fruit production will produce food more times throughout the year with new knowledge gained.

Personal contact with anyone, anywhere, at a moment's notice using a new type of telephone with batteries that stay charged for decades.

Sea and space exploration will abound. Underwater laboratories with scientists living aboard will explore the sea floor with scientific information and adventure into the unknown.

Real estate laws will allow changes in properties in large cities to permit greater commercial heights, especially in the downtown areas, with new structural designs. It will be necessary to have added support to control its continuous motion.

Prices of commercial properties will soar because of limited sites.

Residential property will be at a premium in the large cities with a ninety percent increase in the cost for the average home.

Affordable distant residences from schools or employment will take time away from hobbies.

The stock market will hit 20,000, with the new advanced technological companies leading the way. Many will combine for greater profits as multiple billion dollar companies will become commonplace.

Automobiles will cost seventy percent more and the driver's seat will be lower or the tops higher to accommodate the taller drivers.

Your automobile could or will be directed by an electronic road map to take you to your desired destination without you having to steer it there. A button will do the trick.

The cost of living will increase at least ninety percent, with salaries dragging behind as usual.

People will spend more time using computers so that it will be necessary for them to take some form of exercise at home on a routine basis to maintain their health.

Overpopulation due to longevity will lead to unsanitary conditions and occasional new epidemics.

Idleness and boredom can lead to anxieties and depression, so that each must find new fields to conquer. Go to different classes. Make new friends so that your time will be well spent and enjoyable.

My Grandson Todd Goldberg's Predictions (Graduated San Diego College with Honors in 1999.)

Personal computer, telephone cable television, and home theater and video games will exist in one machine and be user friendly for children. The Internet and cable will merge into one medium. America Online will file Chapter 11.

Gasoline engines will become extinct due to electric motor innovations.

Divorce rates will decrease and marriages increase. Thus, another fleet of baby boomers.

My Friend Nan Potkin, R.N.'s Predictions

The populace will be so knowledgeable about the human body that the need for physicians and surgeons will be greatly reduced. Medical schools will be seeking students. It is likely that medical knowledge will double every eighteen months.

Products and components will be developed and

manufactured all over the world—maybe the solar system.

Proofreader Alan Simon's Predictions

A leading pharmaceutical company will begin marketing the "Fountain of Youth" compound, developed after research by scientists working on how earthworms regenerate. It will be the most controversial man-made drug ever.

Millennium Predictions 2090 and Beyond

The Millennium Philosopher's Predictions

The increased population will not be as much a problem for the wealthy, as life on other planets will be just a step away in the new scheme of things. Lunch at Mars, dinner at Venus, and perhaps a night at the Space Station Hilton Hotel with the new flying machines will be available by just going through the third or fourth dimension.

There will be no more coins or paper money. All charges will be coded and charged to each one's account.

Tasty foods will be created from minerals and inorganic substances to counteract disease. Many will be retrieved from the ocean.

Medical science will be so advanced that humans will live 200 years, causing overpopulation and eventually migration to other planets.

Women will be fertile and able to give birth at the age of one hundred.

Birth defects, disease, and mental disorders will

be diminished or a thing of the past with advanced genetic engineering.

Seven feet will be the average height of the adult human. This will necessitate the increased size of rooms, furniture, automobiles, flying machines, and, especially, shoes.

High-speed rail will take over small airports.

Automobiles will gradually change into flying machines and be piloted by computers, which will minimize accidents due to human error.

We will master science and use photonic energy to satisfy the power demands of an overpopulated earth. [A pipe dream—and don't sell it short!]

New devices will be developed for the handicapped. Artificial limbs and organs will be available for replacement and renewed health.

Cloned pigs, a product of genetic engineering, will be farmed as "organ donors," "donating" their hearts to cardiac patients searching for a healthy existence.

Longevity will lead to boredom for many. The problem will be to keep the persons entertained with new innovations and curriculums. The industrious will take advanced schooling. Multiple degrees in various subjects for the ambitious will be commonplace and a long life can still be fun.

Time will weigh heavily on the lazy and infirm individuals with extended life spans. Depression will be a continuous "normal" symptom for many, posing a dilemma for the psychiatrists.

The infirm, often with minimal funds or available nursing care to aid, will be a long-time medical unsolved and formidable problem to the populace.

Unfortunately, many of the elderly sick will live a very long time, often alone for decades, which will prolong their miseries and hopelessness. The infirm will be irritated, unmanageable, and costly to the society.

Many will wish for death, and suicides may become quite common and acceptable for the lonely and chronically ill. You, the survivors, will have to contribute to their support.

Idleness will be an aged disease of grand dimensions without an answer.

Overpopulation will lead to unsanitary conditions and frequent decimating epidemics.

Death may be a welcome means to many ill for extended periods of time.

Cemeteries will disappear because of the multitude of peoples needing survivable land. Cremation will be commonplace.

Schools will be aplenty to accommodate the aged and industrious; however, there will be a shortage of well-trained and qualified instructors.

The have-nots and those with criminal tendencies will stress the police department. I say it again now, as I said in my *a-Word* book, "Eliminate guns, except for the military."

Airplanes will be powered by nuclear cold-fusion for a ride to outer space.

There will be residences on the various planets

for a change of environment and a vacation away from planet Earth.

Water will be used as a fuel without destroying the atmosphere.

Hydrocarbons have increased on the Earth, an end product of gasoline. They cannot escape due to the sun's rays, which allow them to build up. As a result, the Earth's temperature will rise one degree from the heat, which can cause the oceans to rise and could inundate our shores.

My Good Friend of Sixty Years George M. Cohn, Esq.'s Predictions (age 93)

There will be intermarriage of the various cultures to a great extent, and the now-dominance of the white population will no longer be the majority in the United States. It will be more democratic and considerably less bigoted.

Epilogue

Terrorists hijacked American planes September 11, 2001.

Two planes crashed the two World Trade Centers in New York City, another suicidal plane crashed the Pentagon in Washington, D.C.

More than five thousand dead.

How tragic.

Where was "God"?

My Thoughts Now That I Am Alone

When I see you, my beloved,
I will have changed and so will you.
I will have grown,
Experienced a new lifestyle,
Be more understanding,
Thoughtful and generous,
Loving, kind, with a wealth of news to relate to
    you.
Just holding you in my arms would say it all;
My heart would glow and my body quiver
When GOD allows us to be together again;
That must be heaven is my belief,
A place we all will meet in the Forever land.
The living wish they knew of this;
It must be true;
If not. . . .
It is all that I've got and will hold it with me
Until my time will come to prove if I am right or
    wrong.
           C'est la guerre.

E=Mail to "God"

Dear "Almighty,"

You have done a miraculous job

creating man on your beautiful

planet Earth.

For this we are grateful and

accept our responsibility

for our privilege of "life."

We humans are looking for answers.

Why are we here? For what purpose?

What next?

Please fax your answer soon
as we are anxiously awaiting your reply.

Best wishes,

The Earthlings